Steam around Surrey and Sussex

Roy Hobbs

Ian Allan
PUBLISHING

Introduction

The counties of Surrey and Sussex were once served by each of the three pre-Grouping companies that formed the Southern Railway in January 1923 — the London & South Western Railway (LSWR), the London, Brighton & South Coast Railway (LBSCR) and the South Eastern & Chatham Railway (SECR). Of these the LSWR and LBSCR had already (in the early 1900s) embarked upon programmes of suburban electrification, partly to combat the loss of traffic to the electrified tramways but also to provide for increasing commuter traffic. Under their successor this was progressively extended until, by the mid-1930s, it had reached the South Coast resorts of Brighton, Eastbourne and Hastings; by the middle of 1938 the Mid Sussex line to Portsmouth had been converted, completing the upgrading of main lines in the two counties covered here. Plans had already been laid for the electrification of other, secondary routes, but with the outbreak of World War 2 these were suspended, not being implemented until after nationalisation of the railways in 1948.

In 1956 an extensive programme was put in hand to complete conversion of the remaining lines (and associated branches) to the Kent Coast, this being achieved only in June 1961. An indirect consequence was that other routes, including some in Sussex, continued with existing steam power and hauled stock.

The immediate postwar plans of the Southern Railway indicated that among the lines scheduled for electrification was that from Sanderstead via Oxted to East Grinstead and Horsted Keynes, providing an alternative route to Brighton, along with the section from Reigate to Guildford and onward over the already partly electrified route via Ash and Wokingham to Reading. However, with the publication in 1963 of the Beeching Report, intended to stem BR's increasing deficit, this ongoing programme was abandoned, and many secondary and branch lines, especially in Sussex, were scheduled for early closure. Among these was the line between East Grinstead and Horsted Keynes, scotching the idea of an alternative

---

Front cover: 'Schools' 4-4-0 No 30908 *Westminster* clears Wadhurst station with a Hastings-bound express in June 1957. It is heading a mixed rake of narrow-bodied stock, necessitated by the restricted tunnel bores on this route. The 'Schools' were particularly associated with the line until displaced in June 1958 by diesel-electric multiple-units. *K. W. Wightman*

Back cover: Ex-SECR 'H'-class 0-4-4T No 31518 departs Forest Row for Tunbridge Wells on 11 June 1963. Note the neat appearance of this one-time LBSCR station, with gas lamps, SR signs and porter's trolley; also the signalbox, with orderly row of fire buckets. All were set to disappear with the closure of the branch on 2 January 1967. *D. B. Clark*

Previous page: A view of Eridge, recorded in October 1961 and featuring a BR Standard Class 4MT 2-6-4T heading three Maunsell narrow-bodied coaches and a parcels van on a Tunbridge Wells duty. Narrow stock was necessitated here by the fact that some workings had to negotiate the restricted bore of Grove Tunnel, between Tunbridge Wells West (LBSCR) and Tunbridge Wells (SECR) stations.

Photographs are the author's unless otherwise credited.

First published 2008

ISBN (10) 0 7110 3244 0
ISBN (13) 978 0 7110 3244 6

Published by Ian Allan Publishing

an imprint of Ian Allan Publishing Ltd, Hersham, Surrey KT12 4RG
Printed in England by Ian Allan Printing Ltd, Hersham, Surrey KT12 4RG

Code: 0801/B1

Visit the Ian Allan Publishing website at www.ianallanpublishing.com

path to Brighton. However, after several years of protracted negotiations it was agreed that electrification of the South Croydon–East Grinstead section should proceed, this finally being completed in October 1987. Meanwhile the Tonbridge–Hastings line had been electrified by May 1986, whilst that between Redhill and Tonbridge was energised in May 1994. In all three cases diesel-electric multiple-units (DEMUs) had replaced steam in the interim. The original route between Eridge and Lewes, now curtailed at Uckfield, is now worked by successor DMUs, of the latest generation, but electrification remains under discussion, the necessary finance still to be approved.

Fortunately, from the mid-1950s many experienced railway photographers turned their hand to the then relatively new medium of colour photography in recording scenes that were unlikely to remain unchanged for much longer. In this album an attempt has been made to include some of the more interesting photographs, taken before these irrevocable changes — especially those prompted by the Beeching Report — took effect. Some lines, for example that between Guildford and Farnham via Tongham, had already ceased to serve as normal passenger routes before the use of colour film became widespread, so, where possible, these are featured on the occasion of enthusiast railtours. I have endeavoured to assemble the broadest selection of material that merited inclusion, featuring both branches and main lines; also included are a variety of locomotive portraits together with shed and station scenes, in order to provide a balanced selection.

Picture order has been arranged broadly anti-clockwise following the main routes (and their various connecting and branch lines) radiating from London. We start with the former LSWR main line from Wimbledon to the Hampshire border, continuing with the Portsmouth Direct line and the mainly SECR routes based on Guildford. These are followed by the LBSCR Mid Sussex, Brighton and Oxted lines, our photographic tour concluding with those of the SECR around Hastings.

For obvious reasons it has not been possible to include every location of interest, but I hope the reader will find this selection rewarding, recalling a time when so much variety could be found on the railways of Surrey and Sussex.

Roy Hobbs
Exeter
October 2007

Acknowledgements

A number of photographers have been kind enough to supply examples of their work, much of which is of considerable rarity. Their assistance has been invaluable, and I should like to extend my grateful thanks for the loan of their now irreplaceable transparencies; those concerned include Michael Allan, David Clark, Alan Jarvis, Jim Jarvis, John Langford, Trevor Owen and Neil Sprinks. My appreciation is due also to David Cross, who supplied a number of slides taken by his late father, Derek, and again to David Clark, for the use of material from the collection of the late Kenneth Wightman. In addition, a number of photographs taken by the late W. M. J. Jackson were provided by his son, Brian.

Reference has been made during the compilation of this volume to a number of well-established sources. Among those which have proved especially helpful are *LBSCR Locomotives*, *SECR Locomotives* and *LSWR Locomotives*, all by F. Burtt and published by Ian Allan in 1946, 1947 and 1949 respectively, and *Great Locomotives of the Southern Railway* by O. S. Nock (PSL, 1987). Also of considerable assistance have been the various Middleton Press publications covering Southern lines, along with relevant material, notably the monthly *Railway Observer*, published by the Railway Correspondence & Travel Society.

Left. Following displacement (by ex-GWR '1366' 0-6-0PTs) from the mineral line between Wadebridge and Wenford Bridge two of the three surviving Beattie 2-4-0 well tanks of 1874/5 were brought up to London to work two commemorative railtours from Waterloo to Hampton Court. Nos 30585 and 30587 are seen passing Wimbledon with the first of these, on 2 December 1962. These locomotives had survived on the tightly curved and lightly laid Cornish branch since transfer from London suburban duties at the dawn of the 20th century, although all had been extensively rebuilt during the intervening years. Fortunately both examples illustrated here survive in preservation — No 30585 at the Buckinghamshire Railway Centre at Quainton Road, near Aylesbury, and No 30587 as part of the National Railway Museum (NRM) collection at York but currently back in Cornwall on the Bodmin & Wenford Railway. *J. M. Jarvis*

Above: Seen passing Raynes Park, 'Lord Nelson' 4-6-0 No 30861 *Lord Anson* has charge of a London–Bournemouth working on 22 August 1960. Introduced by SR Chief Mechanical Engineer Richard Maunsell in 1926, primarily for the heavier London–Dover boat trains, the 'Lord Nelson' design was later improved by the fitting of the Lemaître exhaust, the modification being carried out in 1938/9 and indicated by the wider chimney seen here. By October 1962 the entire class would be withdrawn, Nos 30861 and 30862 *Lord Collingwood* being the last operational examples. The prototype, No 30850 *Lord Nelson*, is another locomotive now in the care of the NRM and has recently been restored to Southern Railway postwar malachite green as SR No 850 for use on main-line excursions. *K. W. Wightman*

Above: Unrebuilt 'Merchant Navy' Pacific No 35005 *Canadian Pacific* heads through Raynes Park on 25 August 1957 with an up West of England express. Designed by SR CME Oliver Bulleid, who had succeeded Maunsell in 1937, the 30-strong class entered traffic between 1941 and 1949, the final 10 being turned out under the auspices of BR. All would be rebuilt in the years 1956-9, the principal alterations being replacement of Bulleid's patent chain-driven valvegear with standard Walschaerts motion and removal of the streamlined casing. No 35005 would be so rebuilt in June 1959, finally being withdrawn in October 1965. Subsequently recovered from Dai Woodham's scrapyard at Barry, it survives today as one of three examples restored to working order. *K. W. Wightman*

Right: Virginia Water, junction of the Reading and Weybridge lines to Waterloo via Richmond, is the location for 'U'-class 2-6-0 No 31625, in charge of a mixed goods bound for Feltham yard on 23 June 1957. Introduced in 1928, the 'U' was a Maunsell mixed-traffic design, the first 20 being rebuilds of his 'River' 2-6-4Ts in the wake of the derailment of one of these near Sevenoaks in 1927. Of the total of 50 locomotives built, four would eventually be rescued from Barry; two, including the example illustrated, are to be found on the Mid-Hants Railway, whilst the other two are currently in the care of the Bluebell Railway in East Sussex. *T. B. Owen*

Rebuilt 'West Country' Pacific No 34013 *Okehampton* passes through Woking with a commuter train for Basingstoke on the evening of 17 August 1966. Of the 110 locomotives constructed, including the similar 'Battle of Britain' series, 60 were rebuilt in the years 1957-61 to a more orthodox layout from Bulleid's original semi-streamlined design. Woking's extensive goods sidings, here occupied by a variety of wagons, have in recent times been used chiefly by Network Rail contractors concerned with permanent-way maintenance. *T. B. Owen*

Depicted in charge of a joint LCGB/RCTS railtour, the 'Midhurst Belle', 'USA' 0-6-0T No 30064 heads from Woking towards Guildford on 18 October 1964. Typical American 'switchers' (*i.e.* shunting locomotives), built in 1942/3, the 14 locomotives of this class were acquired in 1946 from the US Army Transportation Corps, chiefly to replace the ageing ex-LSWR 'B4' 0-4-0Ts then working around Southampton Docks.

Six examples were painted in lined green during 1963/4, four for Departmental use at Ashford and Lancing, but this was one of two employed on pilot work at Eastleigh. Most of the class would be broken up following 'dieselisation', but four would survive to be preserved, and No 30064 can nowadays be found on the Bluebell Railway.

Above: Having passed beneath an example of one of the LSWR's signal gantries that formed part of its pneumatically controlled signalling system on this stretch of the main line, rebuilt 'Battle of Britain' Pacific No 34052 *Lord Dowding* approaches Brookwood station from Basingstoke on 3 October 1964. The train is an up working from Southampton, possibly a boat train; note the restaurant car fourth in the consist. The locomotive was constructed at Brighton in December 1946 as No 21C152 and rebuilt at Eastleigh in September 1958. Its career was to end at Salisbury shed (70E) in July 1967, when steam ended on the Southern Region. *D. B. Clark*

Right: With the exception of the electric 'Brighton Belle' the 'Bournemouth Belle' was the last traditional Pullman service to operate on the Southern Region, being withdrawn upon the changeover to electric traction on 10 July 1967. Rebuilt 'Merchant Navy' Pacific No 35026 *Lamport & Holt Line* is seen with the down train, having just passed Pirbright Junction, on 13 March 1959. Several members of the class would be rescued from Barry scrapyard, a total of 10 cheating the cutter's torch, whilst a further example, No 35028 *Clan Line*, would be purchased direct from BR. At the time of writing only two are in working order, these being No 35028, operational on the main line, and No 35005 *Canadian Pacific*, based on the Mid-Hants Railway; in addition No 35029 *Ellerman Lines* can be viewed as a sectioned exhibit at the NRM, York. *T. B. Owen*

Left: From 1951, under the direction of R. A. Riddles, BR introduced a series of Standard classes, amongst which was a Class 5MT 4-6-0 mixed-traffic design; this was a development of William Stanier's well-known 'Black Five' design for the LMS. Several were allocated to the Southern Region, where they worked alongside the Bulleid Pacifics on the South Western Division until the end of SR steam in July 1967. Seen on a Bournemouth-line duty is No 73155 passing through Deepcut Cutting, near Pirbright, in June 1966. From 1959 some 20 of these locomotives were given names carried originally by Maunsell's 'King Arthur' 4-6-0s, and one such example, No 73082 *Camelot*, can nowadays be found on the Bluebell Railway.

Above: North Camp station, although close to the so-named army barracks at Aldershot, in Hampshire, was just inside Surrey and so merits inclusion here. Maunsell 'N'-class 2-6-0 No 31868, of Redhill (75B) shed, calls with a Reading–Redhill service in July 1963. Whilst signalbox, signals and the shelter on the up platform have long since disappeared, the original station building, complete with refreshment room, on the down side remains extant. However, the level crossing (seen here immediately behind the train) has been replaced by an overbridge to the north.
T. B. Owen

One of three such locomotives then based at Redhill, 'S15' 4-6-0 No 30836 is seen near North Camp on 6 October 1956 with a southbound goods including several cattle wagons, representing a type of traffic that has since been completely lost to the railway system. The first 20 'S15s' were introduced by the LSWR under Robert Urie in 1920/1, a further 25, to a modified design by Maunsell, being added by the SR from 1927.

Locomotives from this later series could often be found on passenger work, notably on the regular stopping service between Salisbury and Exeter. Five of the Maunsell engines would ultimately be recovered from Barry, of which No 30847 can be found on the Bluebell Railway, and No 30828 on the Mid-Hants Railway. Two of the earlier Urie locomotives survive at Ropley on the Mid-Hants Railway. *T. B. Owen*

In this wintry scene, recorded on 4 January 1959, 'King Arthur' 4-6-0 No 30795 *Sir Dinadan* approaches Ash with a Reading–Redhill train consisting of Maunsell narrow-bodied set 188. The use of a 'King Arthur' was unusual and arose from the fact that two examples (the other being No 30802 *Sir Durnore*), displaced from Kent in 1958, had been placed in store at Redhill, where increased traffic, notably parcels, in the run-up to Christmas saw them returned to use. Later in 1959 both would be reallocated to sheds on the South Western Division. *T. B. Owen*

Above: In 1899 LSWR CME Dugald Drummond introduced his celebrated 'T9' class of 4-4-0 express-passenger locomotives, which due to their reputation for high-speed running became known colloquially as 'Greyhounds'. The 66 examples built were eventually modified by Urie with extended smokebox, superheating and boiler alterations, as well as having their firebox water tubes removed. No 119 was designated as the Royal engine from June 1935, when it was specially painted in a more elaborate version of SR livery to take HM King George V to the Jubilee Naval Review at Portsmouth; this it retained until 1946, continuing thereafter in malachite green (latterly as BR No 30119) until withdrawal in 1952. Here sister locomotive No 30705 is shown near North Camp with set 558, in carmine and cream, forming a Reading–Guildford working on 23 March 1957. *T. B. Owen*

Above right: Football excursion (or, in railway parlance, 'footex') trains, carrying 'away' fans to matches, were a regular feature of the postwar era. However, over the years patronage declined due to the influence of the private car and the transfer of the remaining traffic to coach operators. Vandalism on these trains also discouraged the railway authorities from continuing their operation; note the toilet roll issuing from the first coach as 'N'-class 2-6-0 No 31401 heads a 10-coach special from Swindon towards Aldershot near Ash on 25 January 1964. This locomotive had probably worked the train through to Guildford from Reading, prior to reversing and heading for its destination via the Aldershot junctions.
T. B. Owen

Right: In their final years the ex-LSWR '700'-class 0-6-0s, also known as 'Black Motors', were employed on various local trip workings and shunting duties. In this scene, recorded on a dull 18 November 1961, No 30325 awaits departure from Farnham goods yard with a pick-up goods including a consignment of sugar beet. Based on a Drummond design of 1897 that closely followed his earlier type for the Caledonian Railway, the '700s' were from 1921 updated by Urie to the condition seen here. One of two allocated latterly to Guildford shed, No 30325 would be among the last seven survivors, all of which were taken out of service in December 1962.

Above: As an Aldershot-bound '2-BIL' electric unit approaches Ash station, visible in the distance, 'N'-class 2-6-0 No 31869 heads towards Guildford with a goods train on 21 April 1956. Of 80 locomotives built between 1917 and 1934, 50 were assembled from parts manufactured at Woolwich Arsenal (hence the 'Woolworth' nickname) and boilers supplied by the Glasgow-based North British Locomotive Co, the sole survivor being No 31874, nowadays preserved on the Mid-Hants Railway. A further 27 kits were acquired by the Great Southern Railway in Ireland, 26 being constructed as GSR Classes K1 (20 locomotives) and K1a (six), approximating to the SECR/SR 'N' and 'U' classes respectively, albeit built to Ireland's 5ft 3in gauge. Six incomplete sets of parts were taken by the Metropolitan Railway, these forming the basis of 2-6-4Ts which eventually passed to the LNER, the last two survivors being withdrawn in 1948. *T. B. Owen*

Right: Maunsell 'U'-class 2-6-0 No 31622 passes Ash Junction on 15 June 1963 with a Reading–Guildford service. The single line visible on the left was once the direct line from Guildford to Farnham, closed to passengers in July 1937 following electrification of the route via Aldershot; it remained as a goods siding, serving mainly the gasworks at Tongham, until closed completely on 1 January 1961. By now No 31622 had been fitted with a chimney of BR Standard design, various front-end modifications having been carried out during a visit to Ashford Works. *T. B. Owen*

Below: Tongham station is the location for this photograph, recording the visit by the Railway Enthusiasts' Club (REC) with the 'Compass Rose' railtour on 5 October 1957; 'M7' 0-4-4T No 30051 is seen attached to ex-LBSCR pull-push set No 721. This enterprising society had arranged for the train to visit various goods spurs and military lines (mainly in Hampshire) that were due for early closure. Tongham had become a goods terminus following withdrawal of the passenger service, the section onward to Farnham Junction being lifted in 1954, and this was the final passenger working over the truncated line prior to complete closure. *T. B. Owen*

Right: Pausing with a Reading–Redhill service, 'Schools' 4-4-0 No 30929 *Malvern* is seen at Guildford on 20 September 1962. This was one of 20 such locomotives fitted with the Lemaître multiple-jet blastpipe, as indicated by the large-diameter chimney. A number of the class had been transferred to the Central Division for secondary duties following displacement of steam from the South Eastern Division in June 1959, but all surviving examples, including No 30929, would be condemned in December 1962. Guildford station would be completely rebuilt in the late 1980s, an official 'reopening' being performed by the Bishop of Guildford in December 1989; of the infrastructure visible here only the footbridge in the background (left) survives. *Alan Jarvis*

A scene of activity at Guildford locomotive shed (70C), recorded on 5 September 1965, just over a year before its official closure to steam (in January 1967). Simmering outside is 'U'-class 2-6-0 No 31619, while within its dark recesses can be discerned a variety of locomotives, including a further Maunsell Mogul and the shed pilot, 'USA' 0-6-0T No 30072, to the left of the small Drewry diesel that had presumably replaced it on such duties; No 30072 would subsequently be purchased privately and can nowadays be found on the Keighley & Worth Valley Railway in Yorkshire. The entire shed site at Guildford is now occupied by a multi-storey car park, whilst the coal road and associated sidings have been replaced with tarmac to provide parking for the city's growing commuter population.

Around 60 years of 0-6-0 development are represented by this view of ex-LSWR '700' No 30698 of 1897 piloting SR 'Q1' No 33022 of 1942, the pair being seen in charge of a Sunday engineering train at Peasmarsh Junction, Shalford, on 25 January 1959. Introduced by CME Dugald Drummond and based broadly on his 1883 'Standard Goods' design for the Caledonian Railway, the 30 locomotives of the '700' class were constructed in Glasgow by Dübs & Co; all were later rebuilt by his successor, Robert Urie, with larger, superheated boilers and extended smokeboxes incorporating a stovepipe chimney. The 40 Bulleid 'Q1s' represented the final design of this wheel arrangement in Britain and were the most powerful examples built; their unorthodox appearance arose mainly from wartime restrictions on the use of materials, but their reduced weight gave them a wide route availability, and they could often be found on a variety of passenger work in addition to their usual goods duties.
T. B. Owen

Above: A further view of the REC's 'Compass Rose' railtour of 5 October 1957, this time having just cleared Farncombe station, on the Portsmouth main line, and about to divert onto the short spur for Godalming goods depot. The latter had been the town's first station, opened in 1849, but upon the completion of Farncombe closed to passengers in May 1897, thereafter remaining open solely for goods traffic until January 1969. The crossing gates seen here would be replaced by lifting barriers in 1975, Farncombe signalbox then being rendered redundant and replaced by CCTV, coloured lights (controlled from a panel at Guildford) having been introduced in 1965. *Neil Sprinks*

Right: Having arrived with a ramblers' excursion from Victoria, Maunsell 'Q'-class 0-6-0 No 30549 waits at Cranleigh, on the line to Christ's Hospital, prior to returning to Guildford on 25 June 1961. This particular locomotive had been fitted in 1955 with a stovepipe chimney as part of draughting experiments to improve the type's notoriously poor steaming characteristics; Bulleid had earlier modified all 20 examples by fitting the Lemaître multiple-jet blastpipe, but this met with only partial success. Following the experiments with this locomotive a further six received similar front-end modifications, this time incorporating a Standard-design single chimney, which would appear to have achieved the desired improvement. One outcome of this was that No 541, which survives on the Bluebell Railway, was similarly modified in preservation.

The final passenger train over the Guildford–Christ's Hospital line — the last leg of the LCGB's 'Wealdsman' railtour of 13 June 1965 — leaves Baynards for Guildford behind 'Q1' 0-6-0s Nos 33006 and 33027. The gate on the right of the picture gave access to a private siding used primarily for the delivery of sulphur to a local earthworks, this remaining open until closure of the line. Opened with the line in October 1865 (and once noted for its extensive display in season of dahlias), Baynards station was built on behalf of Lord Thurlow of Baynards Park, through whose land the line passed; there were otherwise only a few cottages and farms in the immediate locality. The 'Wealdsman' tour, which also traversed other lines scheduled for closure, was blessed with excellent weather, and the tiny 'Thurlow Arms' nearby very quickly ran out of refreshments during the extended photo-stop here!

Right: A further view along the line between Guildford and Christ's Hospital, showing Class 2MT 2-6-2T No 41287 departing Baynards for Horsham on 12 June 1965 — the final day of public operation. No 41287 was to remain in service until July 1966, when it was withdrawn at Eastleigh (70D) shed. Four of these locomotives survive in preservation, whilst a similar '2MT' 2-6-2T to the later (but now extinct) BR Standard design is currently being created at the Bluebell Railway from tender-less Standard Class 2MT 2-6-2 No 78059, recovered from Barry in May 1983.

Right: Heading a three-coach motor set comprising two ex-SECR vehicles sandwiching one of LBSCR origin, 'H'-class 0-4-4T No 31512 passes Christ's Hospital 'B' signalbox on a Brighton–Horsham duty in the summer of 1960. The station here, at the junction with the line from Shalford (Peasmarsh Junction), was especially large and spacious, having been built by the LBSCR to serve the well-known 'Bluecoat' school following its decision to move from London in 1902. However, it remained something of a white elephant, as the majority of pupils were boarders, rendering such extensive facilities largely redundant, and the building was demolished in 1972. *Derek Cross*

Above: On 6 February 1955 the RCTS ran its 'Hampshireman' railtour to mark the impending closure of the Midhurst–Petersfield and Meon Valley lines. For the former leg ex-LBSCR 'E5X' 0-6-2Ts Nos 32576 and 32570 were attached at Horsham, where the train is seen awaiting departure. These two locomotives would be the last survivors of their class, having been rebuilt from 'E5s' in 1911 using boilers of 'C3'-class 0-6-0 design. Only four were so treated, the rebuild showing little improvement in performance over the original. No 32576 would be condemned in July, No 32570 surviving until January 1956. The lines on the right of the picture were used for berthing EMU stock, as here beneath the station footbridge. *J. M. Jarvis*

Right: A nicely prepared ex-LBSCR 'K'-class 2-6-0 No 32353 heads north through Partridge Green with the RCTS 'Sussex Special' railtour of 7 October 1962. The 17-strong class was introduced by Locomotive Superintendent L. B. Billinton in 1913, mainly for express goods work, but latterly could often be seen on passenger duties, especially during the summer months, notably on such turns as the inter-regional trains from the Sussex coast via Kensington or Redhill to destinations in the Midlands. As a result of a BR accounting move to reduce the number of steam locomotives in service the class was condemned *en bloc* at the end of 1962, despite the fact that three examples, including No 32353, had completed less than two years' service since major overhaul. The 'Ks' were popular with crews, but sadly their early withdrawal precluded the possibility of any surviving in preservation. *T. B. Owen*

On a suitably damp and miserable day Redhill-based 'N'-class 2-6-0 No 31866 leaves Partridge Green, on the line between Christ's Hospital (Itchingfield Junction) and Shoreham, with a final southbound railtour on Sunday 5 December 1965. Closure to all traffic north of Beeding Cement Works would be effected on Monday 7 March 1966, the final working being a special van train in the early hours to remove station furniture. The line south to Shoreham Junction would remain open until May 1980 for cement-works traffic.

Representing one of three designs introduced postwar by LMS CME H. G. Ivatt, the Class 2MT 2-6-2Ts numbered 130 locomotives, of which 30 (Nos 41290-319), built by BR following nationalisation, were initially allocated to the Southern Region. They were used, mainly on branch-line work, from Kent to Cornwall, replacing a number of pre-Grouping designs. With the South Downs as a backdrop, No 41303 approaches Shoreham Junction with a Horsham-Brighton train in April 1964. This service had earlier been the province of ex-LBSCR 'E4' 0-6-2Ts but was also notable for being worked by the last 'D3' 0-4-4T, No 32390, until its withdrawal in September 1955.

Above: Heading for the Pulborough–Midhurst branch, the RCTS/LCGB 'Midhurst Belle' railtour of 18 October 1964 is seen shortly after departure from Christ's Hospital behind Maunsell 'Q' 0-6-0 No 30530; this was another of the six examples with BR-design chimney, to which reference is made on page 24. This was the final passenger working over this branch, which was to close to all traffic with effect from 20 May 1966. However, No 30530 would be withdrawn just two months after the tour, in December 1964, its final allocation being Nine Elms (70A) shed.

Right: Photographed on 28 August 1961, ex-LBSCR 'C2X' 0-6-0 No 32441 stands at Petworth, on the branch from Pulborough (Hardham Junction) to Midhurst, with the regular pick-up goods before returning to Pulborough. Given the remoteness of this country station, goods traffic was considerable and included domestic coal, as well as bulk Canadian grain for the nearby flour mill. Passenger services had been discontinued from February 1955, but goods would continue until 20 May 1966, a BR/English Electric diesel shunter working the last train. No 32441 was to remain in service only until October 1961, its final shed being Three Bridges (75E).
W. M. J. Jackson

Below: A pair of ex-LBSCR 0-6-2Ts, 'E4' No 32503 and 'E6' No 32417, double-head the LCGB 'Sussex Coast Limited'— the penultimate passenger working along the Pulborough–Midhurst branch — away from Selham on 24 June 1962. The loss of regular passenger trains some seven years previously was unsurprising given the sparsely populated countryside through which the line passed; in 1938 the inhabitants of Selham numbered just 65. Despite this there was a reasonable level of goods traffic, the village seeing regular milk trains as well as despatching considerable quantities of chestnut fencing, this amounting to 750 tons in 1937. However, the postwar years witnessed a decline, the yard eventually closing in May 1963.

Right: In the fading light of an autumn evening 'Q' 0-6-0s Nos 30543 and 30531 make a final journey over the Lavant branch, being seen shortly after leaving Chichester with the LCGB 'Hayling Farewell' tour of 3 November 1963. The branch was the surviving stub of the line that once ran north to Midhurst, on which passenger services had ceased as early as July 1935. Goods continued until November 1951, being suspended that month after 'C2X' 0-6-0 No 32522 was derailed by a collapsed culvert near Singleton. The line was initially cut back to Cocking, but in August 1953 it was further shortened to terminate at Lavant, the remaining section being required for sugar-beet and, later, aggregates traffic. Final closure would come in March 1991.

With a number of EMUs stabled in the station's extensive sidings, 'Schools' 4-4-0 No 30926 *Repton* leaves Tattenham Corner with the empty stock of the Royal Train that has just brought HM The Queen and her party to Epsom racecourse for the 1962 Derby meeting. The leading carriage is Pullman car *Isle of Thanet*, the second being ex-NER Queen's Saloon No 396 of 1908. The train will return empty to London; as many will be aware, the monarch usually makes the return journey by road. Following withdrawal in December 1962 No 30926 would be overhauled at Eastleigh and exported to the USA, being based initially at the Steamtown Museum in Vermont but used for a time on the Cape Breton Steam Railway. Repatriated to the UK in 1989, it is currently to be found on the North Yorkshire Moors Railway.

With an empty '4-SUB' EMU making for the carriage sidings and the semi-detached houses of Purley visible through the distant haze, rebuilt 'Battle of Britain' Pacific No 34087 *145 Squadron* (minus nameplates) passes the platforms and signalbox — all since demolished — at Coulsdon North with a final steam tour over the SR's Central Division, the LCGB's 'Surrey Downsman' of 5 March 1967. Also visible (and, again, long since removed) is Smitham signalbox, on the Purley–Tattenham Corner branch. The special is heading for Redhill, where it will continue its journey to Guildford on the Reading line before returning to London via a round-about route including Epsom, East Putney, Kensington and Crystal Palace.

Left: Against the backdrop of St Anne's Residential Home (since replaced by a housing estate) BR Standard Class 4MT 2-6-4T No 80139 shunts the Post Office parcels bay at Redhill during October 1963. Rail-based postal traffic at Redhill would finally cease in the mid-1990s, being transferred to a new road/air facility at Gatwick Airport.

Below left: Only recently released from Ashford Works following overhaul in June 1958, 'L'-class 4-4-0 No 31760 stands on the turntable at Redhill before taking up its return working to Tonbridge. Intended to cope with increasingly heavy summer traffic and numbering 22 locomotives, the class was introduced in 1914 by Maunsell, who had just taken over as Locomotive, Carriage & Wagon Superintendent of the SECR from Harry Wainwright, under whose direction the drawings had been prepared. Perhaps surprisingly, given the deteriorating relations between Britain and Germany, it was decided to order 10 of the locomotives from Borsig, of Berlin; frames and boilers were shipped separately to Dover, assembly being completed at Ashford by Borsig staff in June and July 1914. The remaining 12 locomotives were built by Beyer, Peacock & Co, of Manchester, in August and September; the first of these, No 31760 would be retired in June 1961, officially from Nine Elms shed.

Right: Featured previously (page 15) in charge of a Reading–Redhill passenger train, 'King Arthur' 4-6-0 No 30795 *Sir Dinadan* is seen here shunting Redhill up yard in February 1959. Originally attached to a six-wheel tender for working on the Central Section, with its smaller turntables, the locomotive had by this time gained the longer, eight-wheel version common to the majority of the class. Shortly after this photograph was taken it would be transferred to Feltham (70B) shed, eventually being withdrawn at Basingstoke (70D) in July 1962.

Below right: In the postwar era a regular weekday turn between Reading and Redhill, usually the 6.50am from Reading and 11.20 return, was worked by a Western Region locomotive and crew. This was in order to maintain route knowledge, as during the summer months many coastbound holiday trains from the Midlands were worked by WR crews as far as Redhill, where in the late 1950s, at the height of the season, as many as five WR locomotives — generally '43xx' 2-6-0s but occasionally 'Manor' 4-6-0s — could be found on shed. Here '43xx' No 6337 arrives with the 6.50am from Reading, formed of Maunsell set No 957, during July 1962.
K. W. Wightman

Left: An interesting view of the rear of Redhill (75B) shed, recorded on 15 August 1959. Among the locomotives present are Maunsell Moguls and 'schools' 4-4-0s, while on the right of the picture is a BR/English Electric diesel shunter arriving with a train of sand hoppers from the nearby Holmethorpe sidings. Between the shed and the line of wagons occupying the up sidings can be seen the line to Guildford, while just discernible in the background, further up the line towards the station, is Redhill 'B' signalbox. The locomotive shed had been rebuilt by the Southern Railway in 1928, the original SER structure having been erected in 1853.
K. W. Wightman

Above: Following the almost complete eradication of steam traction from the Reading–Redhill and Redhill–Tonbridge lines all passenger workings were taken over by diesel-electric multiple-units (DEMUs); these were to become generally known as 'Tadpoles', on account of their being formed of two narrow-profile 'Hastings' coaches and a full-width driving trailer. On Sunday 3 January 1965, the last day of the old order, the LCGB ran a section of its 'Maunsell Commemorative' railtour from Redhill to Tonbridge, seen here in soft winter light east of Redhill. In charge is Maunsell 'N'-class 2-6-0 No 31411, which had been beautifully prepared by Frank Heritage and his colleagues at Redhill depot.

Left: Displaced from the South Eastern Division by electrification, a number of 'Schools' 4-4-0s were transferred to the Central Division, and in April 1960 three (Nos 30914-6) were allocated to Redhill for local passenger work. Upon completion in June 1961 of the Kent Coast modernisation scheme they were joined by further examples, including No 30930 *Radley*, seen departing Reigate for Reading in June 1962. Since this photograph was taken this location has seen a number of alterations, the crossing gates having been replaced with automatic barriers, and the station house demolished; however, the building on the up side survives (complete with canopy), as does the signalbox, which now controls colour lights as well as

what is today an extremely busy crossing on the A217, a main route to Gatwick Airport and a feeder to the M25 motorway.

Above: In charge of an inter-regional holiday train returning from the South Coast, WR '43xx' 2-6-0 No 7331 speeds through Betchworth during the summer of 1962. One of 20 of this series built in 1932 as Nos 9300-19 and fitted with side-window cabs, this locomotive (originally numbered 9309) would be retired in 1962, but sister No 7325 (9303) survives in preservation on the Severn Valley Railway, having been rescued from Barry in August 1975. *K. W. Wightman*

With the escarpment of the North Downs as a backdrop, 'Schools' 4-4-0 No 30930 *Radley* approaches Gomshall on 25 August 1962 with a Margate–Wolverhampton service. Introduced by Maunsell in 1930 specifically for the London–Hastings route, the 'Schools' were also employed on pre-electrification Portsmouth-line services. This locomotive was another of the 20 examples modified with the Lemaître exhaust, as first fitted by Bulleid to the 'Lord Nelson' 4-6-0s in a bid to improve steaming. All 40 would be withdrawn by the end of 1962, following completion in 1961 of the Kent Coast electrification and a short spell on secondary duties, mainly in Surrey and Sussex. Of the three examples preserved No 30928 *Stowe*, restored as SR No 928 in postwar lined malachite green, can be found on the Bluebell Railway. *K. W. Wightman*

Another view at Gomshall, again on 25 August 1962, this time featuring 'U'-class 2-6-0 No 31631 on a Reading–Redhill duty. The Standard-design chimney reveals that front-end modifications have been carried out, these being effected at Ashford Works in October 1960, but the locomotive would nevertheless be withdrawn in September 1963, its final shed being Guildford (70C). The modern signalbox visible in the distance replaced an earlier SER structure damaged by enemy action during World War 2; following closure in December 1980 it would be taken over by the Permanent Way Department. *K. W. Wightman*

Left: In the spring of 1955 10 examples of BR's Standard Class 4MT 2-6-0, Nos 76053-62, were delivered new to Redhill shed, where they replaced a number of Maunsell three-cylinder 'U1' 2-6-0s. The '4MT' was a development by R. A. Riddles of the similar LMS design introduced in 1947 by H. G. Ivatt. Here, on 15 August 1959, No 76058 climbs Chilworth Bank with a rake of main-line stock in the early BR carmine and cream colours; the train is the 10.37 Saturdays-only Reading–Margate, which operated for a limited period during the summer of 1959. *K. W. Wightman*

Above: The Quarry line between Coulsdon and Earlswood, which opened to passengers in April 1900, was built by the LBSCR to bypass Redhill, thereby avoiding conflict with the rival SECR, which gave preference to its own trains at that location. Pictured in August 1962, Maunsell Mogul No 31825 has just passed Earlswood signalbox and is approaching Redhill Tunnel with a returning inter-regional holiday train that will reach the LMR via the West London line through Kensington Olympia. The extensive sidings on the left have since given way to a housing development.

Photographed on 12 June 1963, 'Q1' 0-6-0 No 33030 shunts a short freight at Salfords, on the London–Brighton main line, once the location of an aviation-fuel terminal supplying the needs of nearby Gatwick Airport. Aside from their regular goods work the 'Q1s' could be found periodically on branch and secondary passenger trains. The prototype, No 33001, survives in preservation and has been restored as SR No C1 — its original identity under Bulleid's numbering scheme; having spent some 27 years (1977-2004) on the Bluebell Railway, where it operated from time to time, it is currently to be found on display at the National Railway Museum in York. *D. B. Clark*

Frequent excursion traffic from other BR Regions to South Coast resorts was a regular feature of Sunday operation in the postwar era, and ex-LMS 'Black Five' 4-6-0 No 45434 is seen here passing Salfords signalbox with one such working in June 1963. Other recorded workings originating from the LMR include one from Luton in 1958 behind a Class 4F 0-6-0, whilst the prohibited 'Jubilee' 4-6-0 type appeared at least twice; on such occasions the offending locomotive would be impounded by the SR authorities and would have to return home light-engine. The ER's 'B1' 4-6-0s also put in occasional appearances, one being noted in August 1960 on the 'City of Leicester Holiday Express'. Use of steam power ceased after 1964, when diesel locomotives or DMUs took over.

Left: Ex-SECR 'H'-class 0-4-4T No 31544 draws into Rowfant station on a Three Bridges–East Grinstead pull-push working during September 1962. This distinctive station was constructed on behalf of landowner Curtis Lampson, an American fur-trader who had made the land available to the LBSCR in 1855; an additional loop and platform were added in 1900/1 along with a footbridge that would subsequently be removed. No 31544 was to remain in service until September 1963, when it was withdrawn at Three Bridges (75E) shed.

Below left: At the beginning of 1963, due to availability problems with the regular 'H' and 'M7' 0-4-4Ts, it became necessary on some services between Oxted or Three Bridges and Tunbridge Wells to use Standard Class 4MT 2-6-4Ts; not fitted for motor working, these had to run round at the end of each journey. Here No 80087 leaves a snow-covered Rowfant for East Grinstead during February 1963.

Right: Grange Road station, between Crawley Down and Turner's Hill, provided both communities with a rail service on the Three Bridges–East Grinstead line. Departing for East Grinstead on 11 June 1963 is a pull-push train propelled by 'M7' 0-4-4T No 30055; this LSWR type was not as popular with local enginemen as was the ex-SECR 'H'-class 0-4-4T, due largely to the difficulty of oiling the inside motion. The line was to close on 2 January 1967, but sections of the trackbed remain open as the Worth Way for use by walkers and cyclists. *D. B. Clark*

Below: A view of Groombridge station in February 1963, with 'H'-class 0-4-4T No 31551 departing with its Maunsell pull-push set for Tunbridge Wells; unusually the locomotive is running boiler-first to its train. Numbering some 66 locomotives, the 'H' class was introduced by SECR Locomotive Superintendent Harry Wainwright in 1904, chiefly to supplement and ultimately replace the Stirling 'Q'-class 0-4-4Ts (and Wainwright's 'Q1' rebuilds) on London-suburban duties. At the opposite platform a similarly bunker-first Standard Class 4MT 2-6-4T awaits departure towards Eridge. At the time of writing Groombridge is the westerly terminus of the Spa Valley Railway, although redevelopment here has necessitated the construction of a new facility to the west of the original station site.

Right: With a characteristic plume of steam issuing from its safety valves, 'H'-class 0-4-4T No 31263 stands in Groombridge goods yard on 7 August 1963. The locomotive is engaged in shunting a number of mineral wagons, most probably bringing coal for the local merchant. Among the last of its class to remain in service and now the only survivor, No 31263 can currently be found on the Bluebell Railway, restored to its former glory in striking lined-green livery as SECR No 263. *D. B. Clark*

At the end of 1910 LBSCR Locomotive Suprintendent D. Earle Marsh introduced his 'J1'-class 4-6-2T No 325 *Abergavenny*, the first express tank engine built to the Pacific wheel arrangement. It was followed early in 1912 by the similar 'J2'-class No 326 *Bessborough*, constructed under the auspices of Marsh's successor, L. B. Billinton, and employing Walschaerts (rather than Stephenson) valvegear. No further examples were constructed to either design, but both locomotives lasted into the BR era, being employed on various duties, notably passenger workings between London and Tunbridge Wells via Oxted. Here, as Southern No 2326, the former *Bessborough* stands outside Tunbridge Wells West shed on 23 September 1947. Both locomotives would be withdrawn in June 1951. *J. M. Jarvis*

Right: Also seen at Tunbridge Wells West, terminus for several LBSCR lines originating in Sussex, 'E4' 0-6-2T No 32519 engages in shunting duties during 1960. Beyond the locomotive can be seen the distinctive station clock tower, and to its left the locomotive shed. Following closure in July 1985 the station was converted into a restaurant, the yard being taken over by Sainsbury's for redevelopment as a supermarket. The shed area has been adapted as the headquarters and easterly terminus of the aforementioned Spa Valley Railway, which intends ultimately to reopen the line west of Groombridge to link up with the Uckfield branch north of Eridge. *Derek Cross*

Below: Awaiting its next duty, ex-LBSCR 'C2X' 0-6-0 No 32525 stands on shed at Three Bridges during October 1961. The 'C2X' class comprised 45 locomotives, these being Marsh rebuilds of predecessor R. J. Billinton's 'C2' class of 1893. The modification work was extensive, entailing the fitting of a larger boiler, an extended smokebox and a new cab and cylinders, and was carried out over a prolonged period, the earliest conversions being completed in 1908, and the final 14 under the auspices of the SR between 1924 and 1940. By the end of World War 2 only three locomotives survived in original form, all being condemned by the end of 1950. Of the rebuilds most remained in traffic until the early 1960s.

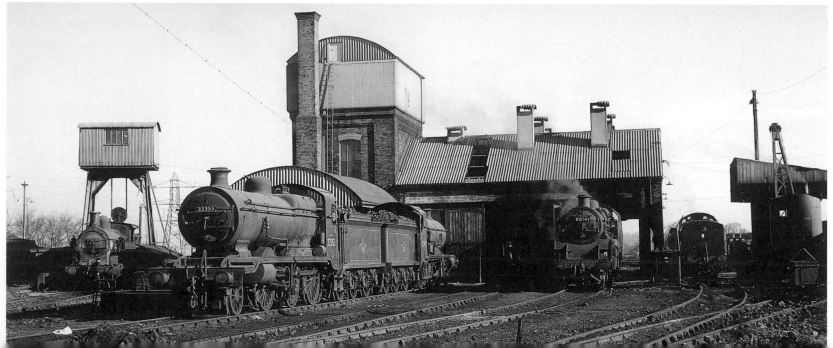

Above left. Seen in the station sidings at Three Bridges, ex SECR 'H' class 0-4-4Ts Nos 31518 and 31551 await departure with a seasonal working, the 2.40pm parcels to East Grinstead, on 19 December 1963. Along with the ex-LSWR 'M7' 0-4-4Ts these locomotives had predominated on pull-push trains to East Grinstead and Tunbridge Wells until June 1963, when DEMUs took over the majority of services. *D. B. Clark*

Left: The rear of Three Bridges (75E) depot in September 1962, with a variety of locomotives including two 'K'-class 2-6-0s, a BR Standard '4MT' 2-6-4T and, beneath the hoist (left), an 'H'-class 0-4-4T; on the right are the coal stage and crane. Situated in the fork of the Brighton and Horsham lines and opened *c*1909, this shed had replaced the original at the south

end of the station and would itself close in June 1964; subsequently used for rolling-stock repairs, it was to survive for a further 10 years before being demolished.

Above: Passing Three Bridges signalbox, unrebuilt 'West Country' Pacific No 34019 *Bideford* approaches the station on 2 March 1963 with what is believed to be a train of empty carriage stock bound for London. Just visible above the train of farm tractors on flat wagons on the other side of the Brighton main line are the signals controlling the line from East Grinstead via Rowfant. No 34019 would survive almost until the end of SR steam, being taken out of service at Nine Elms in March 1967.

Left: With the impending closure of a number of ex-LBSCR branch lines, together with the retirement from the Central Division of the well-known Maunsell Moguls, the LCGB organised an ambitious railtour, the 'Wealdsman', to run on 13 June 1965. Among the lines covered were four branches, two of which were scheduled for immediate closure, and the redundant connection between Polegate and Stone Cross Junction. Here 'N'-class 2-6-0 No 31411 pilots 'U' No 31803 through Cooksbridge *en route* to Haywards Heath; there the train would reverse, being taken onward by rebuilt 'Battle of Britain' Pacific No 34050 *Royal Observer Corps* via Hove, Shoreham and Steyning to Christ's Hospital, where it would reverse again to traverse the line to Guildford before returning to Waterloo.

Right: Comparative views of Brighton (75A) shed, the first, recorded on 13 April 1958, revealing the wide variety of LBSCR designs that could still be found at that time. Among the locomotives visible are examples of the 'E4', 'C2X' and 'K' classes, along with restored Class A1 'Terrier' 0-6-0T No 82 *Boxhill* (latterly Brighton Works shunter No 380S), destined ultimately for the NRM at York; also present are an 'S15' 4-6-0, some ex-LSWR 'M7' 0-4-4Ts and 'T3' 4-4-0 No 563 (now also at York), as restored for the Waterloo Centenary Exhibition of 1948. By contrast the lower view, dating from 27 October 1963, reflects a much-reduced steam allocation, with only the odd Maunsell Mogul, some LMS-designed Class 2MT 2-6-2Ts and BR Standard '4MT' 2-6-4Ts present, along with some diesels — BRCW/Sulzer Type 3s and BR/English Electric shunters. Adding some colour, however, are the Bluebell Railway's Class A1X 'Terrier' No 55 *Stepney* and 'E4' 0-6-2T No 473 *Birch Grove*, being serviced before returning to Sheffield Park with the 'Lancing Bluebelle' railtour.
T. B. Owen (upper)

Left: Ex-LBSCR 'K'-class 2-6-0 No 32341 approaches Hove station on 1 February 1962 with the 1.20pm from Holland Road goods yard. The 'Ks' were a well-established feature of the railway scene in Surrey and Sussex, until their demise in December 1962 being used on both goods and passenger workings. The 17-strong class was constructed between 1913 and 1921; it had been the original intention that the final seven locomotives should be completed as 2-6-2Ts (as the 'K2' class) for express goods work, but in the event they were completed as 2-6-0s, in which form they entered service in 1920/1. *W. M. J. Jackson*

Above: Following the transfer of the LBSCR's carriage works from Brighton to Lancing a special service was introduced in 1919 to convey staff from Brighton to the new location. Soon known locally as the 'Lancing Belle', this train was formed latterly of 10 or 11 coaches of pre-Grouping vintage, the return journey usually being worked by a pair of ex-LBSCR tank engines. In this scene, recorded on 26 March 1962, the evening train is passing Kingston Wharf, Southwick, behind 'E4' 0-6-2Ts Nos 32468 and 32580. The service would cease in July 1964, following the end of steam working in the Brighton area but ahead of the complete closure of Lancing Works in June 1965. *W. M. J. Jackson*

Left: The short Kemp Town branch, opened in 1869, diverged from the main Brighton–Lewes line at London Road (Brighton) station. It was heavily engineered for its length (less than two miles), incorporating both the 14-arch Lewes Road Viaduct and the 1,024yd Kemp Town Tunnel. A round-about route, it suffered inevitable competition from local tram and motor-bus services, this culminating in the withdrawal of passenger workings in January 1933. However, it proved useful for goods traffic, continuing in this rôle until closure in 1971. Here 'E6' 0-6-2T No 32417, having just passed London Road station, returns to Brighton from Kemp Town on 2 October 1962. Nos 32417 and 32418 would be the final examples of their class in service, being withdrawn from traffic at Brighton in December 1962. *W. M. J. Jackson*

Above: The crew of Standard Class 4MT 2-6-4T No 80142, in charge of the 5.06pm Tunbridge Wells–Brighton, patiently await the 'right away' from their guard at Sanderstead on 17 May 1963. The majority of this class, numbering some 155 locomotives, would succumb to the scrapman's torch, but 15 would survive to be purchased by preservation groups, three — Nos 80064, 80100 and 80151 — settling on the Bluebell Railway. Aside from the type's earlier association with this line, the survival of No 80151 seems particularly fortunate, as this was one of the final batch of locomotives constructed at Brighton Works, entering service early in 1957, and for a number of years was allocated to Brighton (75A) shed. *Michael Allen*

Seen shortly after passing Sanderstead an SR Officers' Special, headed by ex-SECR 'D1' 4-4-0 No 31749, heads south to make an inspection tour of several Sussex branches on 25 July 1961. The second vehicle is No DS291, the former LBSCR Director's Saloon, nowadays based on the Bluebell Railway. Introduced between 1921 and 1927, the 21 locomotives of the 'D1' class were Maunsell rebuilds of Wainwright's 'D' type, with modified boiler, new firebox and cab, and piston valves in lieu of the original slide valves. The conversion proved very effective, and these locomotives were extremely popular with crews, some outstanding performances being recorded, notably on the Kent Coast line. Regrettably none would survive long enough to join the ranks of preserved locomotives, the last three, including this example, being withdrawn in November 1961.

Standard Class 4MT 4-6-0 No 75070 is seen about to enter Oxted Tunnel with a racegoers' special returning from Lingfield to Victoria on 25 August 1962. Introduced from May 1951, the '75xxx' series numbered 80 locomotives constructed at Swindon Works and widely distributed among the London Midland, Western and Southern Regions. Lighter than the Class 5MT 4-6-0s of the '73xxx' series, they had an almost universal availability over main and secondary lines. From 1957 some locomotives, including all those allocated to the Southern Region, were rebuilt with a double chimney, as seen here. Fortunately six of the class have been saved, including single-chimney No 75027 on the Bluebell Railway.
John Langford

Left: Shortly after departing Oxted with a Tunbridge Wells motor train, 'H'-class 0-4-4T No 31522 crosses the 150yd Oxted Viaduct, spanning both the A25 road and the River Eden, before plunging into Limpsfield Tunnel. The usual Maunsell two-coach pull-push set has been strengthened by the addition of an older, 10-compartment vehicle of SECR origin. No 31522, constructed in 1908, would eventually be withdrawn from service at Tunbridge Wells West (75F) shed in January 1963.

Below left: Lingfield station on race day, on the same date as the picture on the previous page. On the right, already berthed by 'N1' 2-6-0 No 31822, can be seen the first of three specials run that day. In the foreground is the separate footbridge (later removed and reinstalled at Sheffield Park, on the Bluebell Railway) for racegoers, for whose protection the additional platform canopy alongside was also provided. Lingfield was also noteworthy for its banana-ripening sheds, which received regular traffic, normally from Avonmouth Docks. The 'N1' class comprised just six locomotives, constructed specifically for the London–Hastings line, with its restricted tunnel clearances. *John Langford*

Right: Following the closure in 1958 of the Lewes–East Grinstead line the section south from East Grinstead to Horsted Keynes was retained for emergency use. Only the down line remained operational, the up being used for the storage of condemned wagons; these were cleared gradually over a number of months early in 1960. BR Standard Class 4MT 2-6-4Ts were the usual motive power, but on this occasion the task fell to 'U1' 2-6-0 No 31890, seen passing West Hoathly. Both lines would subsequently be lifted, this being completed by March 1965; somewhat ironically the track-lifting trains were powered by locomotives of the Bluebell Railway, which was later to acquire the trackbed and restore the line as far north as Kingscote. Currently work is underway extending the line further towards the Bluebell's proposed northerly terminus at East Grinstead. *Derek Cross*

LONDON BRIGHTON AND SOUTH COAST RAILWAY Cᵒ

PUBLIC WARNING
NOT TO TRESPASS

Persons trespassing upon any Railways belonging or
leased to or worked by the London Brighton and South Coast
Railway Company solely or in conjunction with any other
Company or Companies are under The London Brighton
and South Coast Railway [Various Powers] Act, 1899, section
15, and are liable on conviction to a penalty of FORTY SHILLINGS
in accordance with the provisions of the said Act
public warning is hereby given to all Persons not to
trespass upon the said Railways

LONDON BRIDGE TERMINUS
OCTOBER 1899.

J. Brewer
Secretary

Left: In charge of an RCTS special on 13 April 1958, ex-LBSCR 'H2' 4-4-2 No 32424 *Beachy Head* approaches Newhaven Town for the last time. Withdrawn shortly afterwards, it was the last survivor of the well-known Marsh Atlantics once used to haul expresses on the Brighton company's system and had by now outlasted its sisters in service by close on 18 months, during which time it could frequently be found on Newhaven Harbour boat trains. Introduced in 1911, the 'H2s' differed only in minor detail from the successful Atlantics designed by H. A. Ivatt for the Great Northern Railway. Regrettably No 32424 would subsequently be broken up, but the Bluebell Railway is currently in the process of building a replica using a GNR Atlantic boiler discovered in East Anglia.
K. W. Wightman

Left (inset): Rare surviving LBSCR Trespass notice, still *in situ* in July 1963 alongside the Newhaven Harbour Tramway.

Above right: Having left the main Newhaven Harbour Tramway, ex-LBSCR Class A1X 'Terrier' 0-6-0T No 32670 runs alongside the A259 road in May 1962 on the short section of line that gave access to the up yard at Newhaven Town. The tramway had been opened in 1879 by the Newhaven Harbour Company, which in 1898 purchased LBSCR 'A1' 0-6-0T No 72 *Fenchurch* (ultimately to become BR No 32636) to facilitate maintenance of the dockside breakwater. The line was subsequently worked by various 'Terriers', No 32678 performing the last rites on its closure in August 1963. Both this and No 32670 would later be purchased privately and can now be found on the Kent & East Sussex Railway.

Right: Reference has been made earlier to the RCTS 'Sussex Special' railtour of 7 October 1962, and in this view 'E6' 0-6-2T No 32418 and 'A1X' 0-6-0T No 32636 (by then the oldest locomotive operational on BR) head the train away from Seaford towards Newhaven on the return leg to Brighton. Following its spell with the Newhaven Harbour Co the 'Terrier' passed to the Southern Railway in 1927 as No B636 (later 2636). Whilst No 32418 would be condemned in December 1962, No 32636 was to see out its BR career on the Hayling Island branch, culminating in closure of that line in November 1963; it was then acquired by the Bluebell Railway and has since been restored to near-original 'A1' condition (with shorter smokebox) as LBSCR No 672.

Left: In charge of a pair of motor sets comprising vehicles of LBSCR and LSWR origin, LMS-designed Fairburn Class 4MT 2-6-4T No 42101 approaches Groombridge Junction on an Eastbourne–Tunbridge Wells duty, probably in the summer of 1959. Some 41 locomotives of this type (Nos 42066-106) were built at Brighton Works from 1950 to 1952, chiefly to replace the ex-LBSCR Class I3 4-4-2Ts of 1907-13, which were fast becoming life-expired following a hectic period coping with London commuter services during World War 2. Sister '4MTs' Nos 42073 and 42085 are now preserved on the Lakeside & Haverthwaite Railway in Cumbria. *Derek Cross*

Above: Eridge, junction of the lines to Eastbourne and Lewes, is the location for unrebuilt 'West Country' Pacific No 34098 *Templecombe*, heading a rake of Maunsell narrow-bodied coaches, plus two vans, forming the 1.55 Brighton–Victoria service during July 1960; the locomotive would later return with the 6.10pm Victoria–Brighton commuter train via East Grinstead. Still attached to the original high-sided design of tender, it would be rebuilt the following February, when the 'air-smoothed' casing would be removed and Bulleid's chain-driven valvegear replaced by the more conventional Walschaerts system. Constructed at Brighton after nationalisation, in December 1949, it would be withdrawn in July 1967 at the end of Southern steam operation. *Derek Cross*

Left: During the final week of steam operation on the Eridge–Polegate route, otherwise known as the 'Cuckoo line', BR Standard Class 4MT 2-6-4T No 80019 on an Eastbourne–Tunbridge Wells working crosses a southbound train at Mayfield. Complete closure between Eridge (Redgate Mill Junction) and Heathfield was to take effect on Sunday 13 June 1965 following the passage of the 'Wealdsman' railtour, the section south from Heathfield remaining open thereafter for goods traffic. A limited passenger service between Hailsham and Eastbourne continued until September 1968, when this too was withdrawn, precipitating total closure of the line north of Polegate, goods traffic to/from Heathfield having ceased the previous April as a result of damage inflicted on an underbridge by a road crane.

Left: 'H'-class 0-4-4T No 31518 pauses at Heathfield on 3 June 1962 with a train for Eastbourne; the appearance of the staff on the platform suggests it may be waiting to cross an up working. Heathfield was interesting inasmuch as it had its own supply of natural gas (discovery of which came as an unexpected bonus in 1896 during test-boring to find a water source), which was used both for station lighting and, by means of a gas-powered engine, for pumping water; however, in 1963 the supply was found to have diminished significantly, and the bore was sealed. The 'Cuckoo line' nickname derived from the town's Cuckoo Fair, held each April. *D. B. Clark*

Further down the 'Cuckoo line' was Hellingly station, which Maunsell 'N'-class 2-6-0 No 31400 is seen departing with a train for Eastbourne on 8 April 1964. This location was noteworthy for its connection with the Hellingly Hospital Railway, which had originated as a 1¼-mile contractors' branch, laid to assist with construction of the hospital in 1899; upon opening of the hospital in 1903 it was acquired by East Sussex County Council, being used to transport coal for the boilers and generators, which in turn provided power for electrification of the branch. This arrangement continued until March 1959, when the hospital changed to oil, and all trace of the branch was subsequently removed, leaving the large open space (seen here on the left) once occupied by the exchange sidings.
D. B. Clark

In 1897 LBSCR Locomotive Superintendent R. J. Billinton introduced his 'E4' class of 0-6-2 radial tanks, designed for mixed traffic use. Remaining in production until 1903, the class eventually numbered 75 locomotives, all named after locations on the Brighton system. Seventy were still in service at the time of nationalisation, following which they continued in use on goods or local passenger work. No 32479 (formerly *Bevendean*) is seen on a Hailsham–Eastbourne turn on 6 June 1962. The final survivors were due to be condemned in December of that year, but frozen fuel lines on their diesel-shunter replacements during the severe winter of 1962/3 saw three examples retained; among these was No 32479, which would be the last of the class to remain in service, finally succumbing in June 1963. Sister locomotive No 32473, restored in Marsh umber as LBSCR No 473 *Birch Grove*, survives in preservation on the Bluebell Railway. *D. B. Clark*

Right: Mention has been made earlier of the passenger work undertaken by Lawson Billinton's 'K'-class 2-6-0s, introduced primarily for express goods duties. Here No 32340 is seen shortly after leaving Polegate on 3 June 1961 with what is believed to be the Eastbourne portion of the Saturdays-only 10.45am Birmingham Snow Hill–Eastbourne/Hastings via Redhill. This was one of a number of inter-regional workings that operated during the currency of the summer timetable until the early 1960s. *W. M. J. Jackson*

Below right: Coupled to its ex-LBSCR twin-coach pull-push, 'H'-class 0-4-4T No 31519 of St Leonards (74E) shed waits in the sidings at Hastings on 15 May 1954. The locomotive is in excellent condition externally, having presumably visited Ashford Works only a short time previously. Displaying the correct disc code and with its coal bunker well filled, it is probably about to undertake duties on the Bexhill West branch from Crowhurst. Constructed in 1908, it would eventually be condemned in February 1961.
T. B. Owen

Below: Anticipating the virtual elimination of steam traction from the South Eastern Division with effect from 12 June 1961, the LCGB ran its 'South Eastern Limited' railtour on the previous day, a Sunday. Here 'D1' 4-4-0 No 31749, piloted by 'H'-class 0-4-4T No 31308, reverses the train onto the KESR branch at Robertsbridge. Class A1X 'Terrier' 0-6-0T No 32662 is out of view at the far end; before proceeding to Tenterden the train would have similar No 32670 attached to the opposite (near) end, replacing Nos 31749 and 31308, which had brought the train from Tonbridge, following earlier visits to the Maidstone West line (by now electrified) and the Hawkhurst branch. The latter, along with the KESR, would be closed from the following day. *John Langford*

Right: KESR Trespass notice still *in situ* at Robertsbridge in May 1965.

KENT & EAST SUSSEX RLY.

PUBLIC NOTICE NOT TO TRESPASS

THE KENT & EAST SUSSEX RAILWAY (AMENDMENT) ORDER, 1917, (SECTION 2), PROVIDES THAT ANY PERSON WHO SHALL TRESPASS UPON ANY LINES OF THE RAILWAY SHALL ON CONVICTION BE LIABLE TO A PENALTY NOT EXCEEDING FORTY SHILLINGS, AND THE PROVISIONS OF THE RAILWAYS CLAUSES CONSOLIDATION ACT, 1845, WITH RESPECT TO THE RECOVERY OF DAMAGES NOT SPECIALLY PROVIDED FOR AND OF PENALTIES AND TO THE DETERMINATION OF ANY OTHER MATTERS REFERRED TO JUSTICES, SHALL APPLY.

ANY PERSON OR PERSONS DAMAGING OR REMOVING ANY PORTION OF THE COMPANY'S PROPERTY WILL BE PROSECUTED.

KENT & EAST SUSSEX RAILWAY,
MANAGING DIRECTOR & ENGINEERS OFFICE.
TONBRIDGE, MARCH 1948.

BY ORDER,
W.H. AUSTEN,
MANAGING DIRECTOR & ENGINEER.

PENALTY FOR DESTROYING OR DEFACING THIS NOTICE, FIVE POUNDS.

Right: The Kent & East Sussex Railway, linking Robertsbridge (Sussex) with Headcorn (Kent), was one of several light railways built in Britain under the management of Col Holman F. Stephens. A variety of locomotives, most second-hand, was used to operate services; here we see ex-LBSCR 'Terrier' No 3 standing outside Rolvenden shed on 24 September 1947. Having entered service with the LBSCR in 1872 as No 70 *Poplar*, it had been passed to the KESR's predecessor, the Rother Valley Railway, in 1901. Acquired in original form as an 'A1', it eventually received an 'A1X' boiler in 1943. The KESR was to lose its independence upon nationalisation of the railways in 1948, No 3 being taken into Southern Region stock as No 32670. Following withdrawal in November 1963 it would return to a revived KESR, based at Tenterden, reverting to its earlier identity as No 3 *Bodiam*. *J. M. Jarvis*

Below right: A further view at Rolvenden, this time recorded following nationalisation and shortly before the withdrawal of passenger services in January 1954. Ex-SECR 'O1' 0-6-0 No 31065, a 1908 Wainwright rebuild of a Stirling 'O'-class locomotive of 1896, stands in front of the engine shed. This machine was regularly allocated to the KESR, being responsible for services over the Tenterden–Headcorn section, whilst a 'Terrier' covered mainly the Robertsbridge–Tenterden workings. By the time of its withdrawal in June 1961 No 31065 would be the last survivor of its class, having been employed in the intervening years on goods work over the remaining portion of the one-time East Kent Railway between Tilmanstone Colliery and Shepherdswell. Subsequently purchased privately for preservation, it is nowadays based on the Bluebell Railway, having been restored to lined-green livery as SECR No 65. *Author's collection*

Left: A typical view at Wadhurst, recorded during June 1957 and featuring 'E1' 4-4-0 No 31507 passing over the foot crossing south of the station with a train for Hastings. The 'E1s' were Maunsell rebuilds of Wainwright's 'E' class of 1905, being modified along similar lines to the 'D'-class locomotives to which reference is made earlier (page 64). Eleven examples were so treated, commencing with No 179 (later SR No 1179 and eventually BR 31179) at Ashford in 1919, the remaining 10 being rebuilt by Beyer, Peacock & Co, of Gorton, Manchester, in 1920. The 'D1s' and 'E1s' were virtually indistinguishable save for the coupling rods, which were smooth on the former and fluted on the latter. *K. W. Wightman*

Above: Rye station, on the Ashford–Hastings line, is the location for this view of 'Schools' 4-4-0 No 30923 *Bradfield* heading the 5.45am London Bridge–Ashford service on 14 April 1962, having worked the train forward to Hastings via Battle. With the end of the steam-heating season diesel traction was scheduled to take over this working the following month. Although threatened with closure in the Beeching Report, the line would be retained and survives today, worked by modern DMUs. No 30923 had originally been named *Uppingham*, but the plates were removed in the face of objections from the school concerned, following which the locomotive was renamed. It would be withdrawn from service at Brighton shed in December 1962. *D. B. Clark*

Index of locations illustrated

With the cow parsley in full bloom, 'H'-class 0-4-4T No 31551 is seen west of Groombridge with a motor train for either Oxted or East Grinstead on 1 June 1963. The auto-set is one of the 20 Maunsell two-coach pull-push units (Nos 600-19) introduced in 1959, each comprising an Open Second and a Corridor Brake Composite, the latter functioning as a driving trailer; these had been converted from main-line stock and replaced sets of mainly SECR and LBSCR origin, all of which had been removed from service by mid-1962. *D. B. Clark*